Whispers & Wanderers

THE VOICES

Shubham Natu

BlueRose ONE.com
Stories Matter

First Published in May 2022

ISBN: 978-93-5628-260-5

BLUEROSE PUBLISHERS

www.BlueRoseONE.com

info@bluerosepublishers.com

+91 8882 898 898

Cover Design:

Geetika

Typographic Design:

Namrata Saini

Illustrations Design:

Priyanka

Distributed by: BlueRose, Amazon, Flipkart

Well, being an ardent reader, I have read this section of a book, 'n' number of times!

Dedicating their book or a piece of art, either to their wife, some friend, kids, parents, etc., many authors and writers have done it and are doing it beautifully!

SO how can I lag? Some traditions need to be followed, right? 😉

So here I am.

Definitely whatever I have achieved or will achieve in my life, be it big or small, I have and will always dedicate to my parents and my family.

But this time, I also dedicate this book, which is my first book, to the different people who came and went at different stages of my life or are still there.

I want this to be dedicated to them as well because they helped me, and some are continuing to do so, consciously or unconsciously, to learn different things in life, to learn and to grow, be it with negative or positive experiences.

If it wasn't for those people in those moments, I probably won't be able to write and share my thoughts, feelings, and experiences via this book, which you are holding.

"Thank you to all my readers, and especially those who are currently holding this piece of work of mine.

I hope it stands true in its real purpose of entertaining you, teaching you, and making you ponder a bit.

Keep showering your love with my work, like you always do.

Looking forward to getting in touch with you and hearing your feedback and suggestions! "

-Your Author

"Life Is A Great Teacher.

We, Just Need To Be Good Students."

EPISODE 1

Yes, Life is a Great Teacher!

Said and conveyed so, by the voices in my head, one fine day.

In our lifetime, we consider life to be many things. If something good happens, we say, WOAH! What a glorious life I have! Everyone should have a life like mine!

If something bad happens, or if we don't get what we want or desire for, we say, why is life being so cruel to me?

Why life is playing like my enemy?!

Trust me, I also felt the same way. In fact, sometimes I still do, but now only sometimes!

As my voices made me aware that I was perceiving life in a bit of a wrong way, as they said:

"You are perceiving life in a wrong way, buddy!

In contrast to what you think of life being a friend or an enemy, life is indeed just a teacher and you, you are just not being a good student all along.

Like a teacher, life will only provide you with what is important for you at that moment. It will punish you sometimes for your deeds, and will also reward you when the time is right.

So, stop thinking of life being your enemy or friend, just be a good student and do your work with dedication and zeal, that's it!"

Definitely, instead of channeling our thoughts and our focus towards blaming or suddenly praising life, if we can channel our thoughts and focus towards the right path, towards our aim and do our work, like a great teacher, Life will also give us rewards, otherwise, Life needs to be that punishment giving teacher, only to bring us back to the right path!

EPISODE 2

Voices in my head
What do you say?
What do you convey?

A sudden urge
A sudden desire
What do you say?

I know!
I understand!
But the consequences,
Consequences
Are bothersome
Consequences
Are loathsome

They trouble me
They hold me
They pull me back

Voices in my head
What do you say?
What should I do?

Want to think less about consequences
But,
What should I do?
They hold me!
They pull me!

A sudden outburst
That's what I seek
What do you say?
Where are you?
Speak up!
What should I do?

Guidance,

We all need guidance at some point of time in our lives.

It's not always like we have someone around us who can share his/her perspective, who can share their thoughts, or who can guide us.

In those moments, our voices can help us, can guide us.

My voices do guide me!

They are like a companion to me, constantly speaking.

These voices sometimes make me do pretty nasty things and sometimes pretty good, but they are always there, floating around, sharing their perspective.

Some might think on reading till now, what he is talking about?

Has he gone crazy?

Well, I do consider myself insane, but only a bit.

If you don't believe me regarding those voices, introspect yourself.

Sit in silence for a while, your voices will certainly greet you!

Some can recognize them and some can't.

Some might call them by other names.

But I named them so, based on Randy Orton's entrance song, which is titled ***Voices in my head***!

If you don't know Randy, well watch WWE.

Even his entrance song goes like this,

I hear voices in my head
They council me, they understand
They talk to me!

See, maybe Randy and I share the same thinking 😉

Sometimes, we ponder way too much before doing anything, we just argue with ourselves, whether we should do it?

What will be the consequences?

And Whatnot!

We just forget to act on impulses in those moments and lose our time in that process, and that too unnecessarily, when this much pondering isn't even required.

In those moments, we need some guidance and that's when we can sync up with our voices, gather some courage, and do the task!

Like we all want to do at some point in time, but aren't able to do so, because of '**Overthinking about the consequences**'

Why don't you leave me alone ???
Ummmm... because I miss you...

EPISODE 3

Have you ever observed the things surrounding us in a different way? In a, say, some special way maybe, like this?

Beneath the open sky
Shines this bloomy flower
Magnificent as always!

Beneath the open sky,
Blooming like never before

But it has to go down one day
Into the oblivion
Only to shine bright again
Under the glittering sun
Drawing its energy
Only to stand up tall again!
To be beautiful again!

Beneath the open sky
I watch it grow
I watch it die
Only to renew again
Giving a positive energy
To stand tall
To fight disparities
To bright up high

Beneath the open sky
I watch a magnificent flower glow
Magnificent as always
Blooming like never before!

Have you ever tried to observe these beautiful things surrounding us, like a flower, with this sort of perspective, with which I did?

Well, I also hadn't, until,

One day while roaming outside my house, voices in my head popped up and asked,

"Hey, do you know the story of a magnificent flower?"

Which, of course, I hadn't, and hence; the voices introduced me to this magnificent flower.

After knowing its story, it made me realize how we can learn from a variety of different things, different animals which are present in our surroundings!

But sadly, we ignore them, and we end up hurting them.

Like this beautiful flower, which one day shines as magnificently as it can, but on another day, either it gets plucked by a human or it dies because of excessive heat or excessive rain.

Despite facing all these challenges, it grows up again, as magnificent as before, maybe even more magnificent, fighting all the challenges, standing strong, and waiting for the next challenge.

It made me realize how we humans succumb to minor difficulties, challenges, and barriers. We fall down a bit and we give up!

Just like that.

But we need to learn from this flower, whom we pluck almost every day, creating a barrier in its journey.

We need to learn from it how to never lose hope, how despite facing challenges, despite falling, we can keep our hopes high, we can bounce back and continue towards our ultimate destination!

Isn't the story magnificent like the flower? 😊

After all, it's like what one of my close friends says…

"It's the little things in life,

Which creates a difference!"

EPISODE 4

Under the hue of the open sky,
Kissed by the breezing wind passing by,
Feels like,
Maybe,
Just maybe
Should steady my wandering mind

Under the hue of the open sky,
With a gentle tap of rainwater falling by,
Feels like,
Maybe
A deep breath
Is awaiting me as a passerby

Under the open sky,
Just want to feel the breeze
And observe the hues of the sky
As they slowly and steadily say goodbye!

We get so engrossed in our day-to-day life, our day-to-day activities, that we forget to feel and observe the little things which are happening around us, the little things which can give us genuine happiness, we just ignore them, and don't enjoy their company!

Similar was the situation with me as well.

That's when my voices introduced me to these little droplets of rain.

They were already there, maybe a few days back, maybe a day before, they were there, but I was not aware how I can really enjoy their presence.

That's when one fine day, my voices, well and truly introduced me to the joy of rain, the pleasure of feeling those water droplets.

That day, during those moments, I forgot about my daily work, the things which were bothering me, and all the other stuff.

I just enjoyed the company of these gentle raindrops!

Similarly, there are many such things, whose presence can provide us joy, can provide relief and peace, whose presence we don't acknowledge.

Once in a while, we should take some time off and enjoy these little things. Spending a few moments with them may help us forget our sorrows and can provide us with a solution for life's complex situations.

"I Moonwalk Out Of
The Problems
Only To Find Out That,
Problems Have Moonwalked
Alongside Me! 😉"

EPISODE 5

If the walls could speak,
I will find solace in them
As my wall would be my bestie,

It will never leave me
It will never hurt me
I will confess everything to my wall
From my happiness to my sorrow
From my love to my hate

People will come and go
But my wall,
My wall will always be there for me

It will tickle me
It Will make me laugh
Will make me cry Even!

But it will always be there
I wish my wall could speak
But just don't leak my emotions
To the outside world!

Whenever I punch it in anger,
Should express its hurt
Otherwise, I would never understand
It's importance
I wish my wall could speak!

I wish I had such a wall, then I would never have to confess to someone and let some of them take advantage of my emotions for their gain.

you got this buddy!!!

"If you really want to...
Use someone's strength, power, money
Even use their intelligence for once
For your own benefit
But,
Never ever use someone's emotions
Just to fulfill your cause
Because
That person might not remain the same afterwards!"

EPISODE 6

"Don't take a chance to walk on that slippery road again.
This time it may end up in a mud puddle!"

Mistakes are acceptable, none of us is 100% perfect, it's okay to commit mistakes, but what is not acceptable,

Is not learning from those mistakes and committing those mistakes again and again.

One time or maybe a few more times, you will survive the hard blows which come like a present as part of the aftermath of those mistakes.

But you cannot survive every time, mark it!

Hence, mistakes are acceptable, but not learning from those mistakes and making the same mistakes, again and again, is reckless!

EPISODE 7

I'm a lost soul
Searching for a cause
Wandering for a cause
Slipping for a cause
Running for a cause
Floating for a cause

For a cause, looking, I'm
But what do I get?
I get an illusion

An illusion
A mirage
But not a proper cause!
But I'm in search of one

I'm not a perfect soul
And never could be

I make mistakes
I recognize my mistakes
Learn from them
Sometimes I'm successful,
Sometimes I'm not!

Need a helping hand
As I'm a lost soul,
Never could I survive alone
Need a helping hand
Who would help me get out!
From an infinite abyss,

I'm a lost soul
Searching for a cause
Floating for a cause
A proper cause!

It's like, easier said than done thing, when we realize our mistakes, acknowledge them and try to work upon them and improve.

Because, when we commit a mistake and realize it, depending upon the magnitude of the mistake, it leaves behind a mark, a pain, which needs to be handled and it's not always easy to handle that pain along with working on those mistakes.

In those moments, we might need some guidance from or via someone.

Maybe we don't always need a fellow being, maybe some inhuman thing, maybe some non-living thing can help us, can inspire us, can motivate us, to stand tall, fight, learn and improve!

"Try To Find The Hidden Meaning
In The Hidden Treasure
Of The Hidden Aspects
Of The Hidden Life Which You Have Got!
So That,
You Know The Hidden You
Inside You!"

EPISODE 8

"Don't come here only when
you need positivity
This is not a monk's grocery shop!"

Well, voices in my head don't always play a cute inspiring goody hero, they do sometimes become a nasty villain, maybe not completely a villain per se,

But they make me realize that it's not always like if you do good to people, they in return will do good to you, or maybe if you do good, they will remember you and stay the same with you always, or something like that.

Some people just stay in touch with you, till their desire or whatever they want gets fulfilled, then they leave you, however selfish it may sound, but it happens, reality dude!

And it's never bad to identify and cut out such people if it provides you peace.

After all, it comes down to,

Looking out for self, right?

EPISODE 9

"Low on energy
Full onn drain
Am I gone fucking insane?"

That's exactly what I feel sometimes! 😉

After working hard, day in and day out, to fulfill my goals and desires, patiently trying to give my best, but that thread holding my patience breaks and I start feeling rusty!

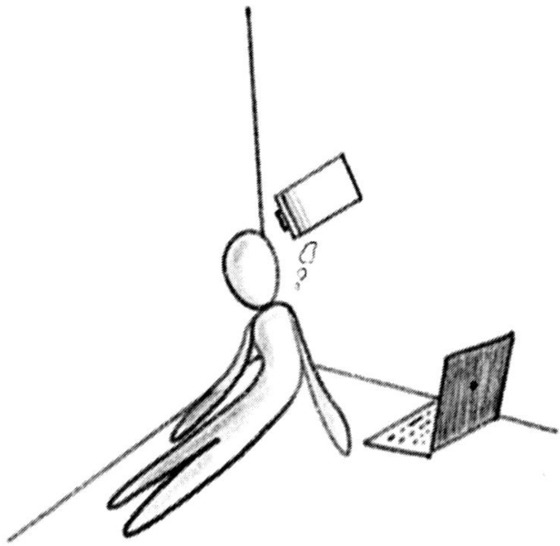

EPISODE 10

It's okay to feel like this sometimes, like giving up everything, just chill out.

But, when it happens frequently, that may be a sign of concern. That's when we need some motivation, some may be friendly cheers, we may need the voices to inspire us again!

And that's what they do, maybe with something like this,

Sun was bright
Like happiness in my life
The moment seemed right
Because I was riding on a tide

But the almighty seemed to pout
And challenges came like a cloud
Shadows depicted my sorrow
As I hoped for a new tomorrow
Shadows seemed depressing
But I felt full-on challenging

I had a fire
To face these sires
So, to ignore this despire
I said,

"Ignoring the shadows
Mesmerized I'm!
Looking at the clouds
Hovering over my beautiful desires
Mesmerized I'm!
As the glowing sun is waiting for me,
To get past this cloudy sky,
Waiting for me is the sun,
in the sky,
Holding my beautiful desires within it
As a friendly alibi!"

EPISODE 11

Just like, after working hard, day in and day out, we feel like relaxing, but we sometimes end up slipping deep into that rest and chill cycle, that we stop working for our goal and desires completely.

Similarly, it happens like we work and work for our goals and desire, but we forget to take out time for ourselves once in a while; we forget to relax, to take in deep fresh air!

That's when we need our voices to remind us,

Don't think too much
Don't feel too much
Sit back and relax dude!

Don't react too much
Don't get attached too much
Sit back and relax dude!

Don't be jealous too much
Don't remain serious too much
Sit back and relax dude!

Feel the air
Feel the freedom
Don't be bound too much
Don't be shy too much
Sit back and relax dude!

Be alert
Remain stiff
But don't forget to enjoy your life dude!

EPISODE 12

You must have come across people saying, *OMG, What an ODD Day it is!*

Or you, yourself, might use it frequently.

It comes out of us, when even day-to-day activities go wrong or seem difficult or even what we love to do, we don't feel like doing it!

It's okay, as a human, everyone comes across this odd day, once in a while.

As we just talked about taking a rest day a little while ago, a relaxing day from everyday hard work schedule, so is true, when we talk about one odd day.

Sometimes, when this odd day comes across, we end up thinking about it so much so that we start feeling anxious about it, we get restless!

That's when we need to realize,

It's just one odd day!
Not every day is the same my friend,
It is just one odd day

It is just about one odd day
When you walk over a banana peel and fell off
It is just about that one odd day!
You shouldn't feel sad and stop taking that road again
Was just a matter of one odd day

It was a day
When like everyday
You planned to study
But you couldn't!
Don't feel depressed
It is just one odd day
Take rest and come back strong
It's all about that one odd day

You wished to switch off the fan
But ended up switching off the main power supply of the system!
Not in the mood?
Sit back and relax
Nothing to be ashamed of

It's just about that one fine odd day

No one is perfect
No one is born champ
Even great leaders to which you look up to,
Faced an odd day!

And you,
You, my friend, are still a work in progress!
Have your odd day
Enjoy it
Plan your not-so-odd days on that cute little odd day!
Introspect!
And come back strong
Nothing to fear about
Nothing to be bothered about
Everyone faces an odd day
So shall you!

It's okay to have one odd day. As a human, it's bound to happen.

Nothing to be bothered about.

Instead, we can utilize that one odd day, to do some other things which we like, like, we can plan for the days following that odd day, we can introspect on our past events and can think of how we could have performed better and learn from it, or simply we can relax!

But just like relaxation days, we should keep in mind, these odd days should not happen frequently, otherwise, something is really wrong and we need to work on getting back on track again!

EPISODE 13

Just imagine, whatever your desires are, you have fulfilled those, and you are living in that moment of glory!

It's fascinating and provides you with a new source of energy.

Isn't it? 😉

The time was right
To begin the fight,
Nervous at the start,
But fire inside my heart!

The time was right
To begin the fight,

Just remain smart
Said my heart,

The path was tough
Full of thrones!
Some pricked my leg,
Some of my legs survived!

Yeah, for sure
The struggle was there,
Eminent, it seemed!

Life felt short,
Yeah, it felt
Life is short!

The moment also came
When quiet was profound!
Everything seemed like
An uphill struggle
Legs broke
Hands fumbled.
The body gave up!

Yes, right,
Body gave up
As it was an uphill struggle!
Then a voice inside me reverberated
Profoundly, it reverberated!

Just think of the view from the top
It spoke
One time struggle
Dear friend,
Lifetime gain!

The heart rejoiced
Hearing the voice,
Like water in a long desert
Was That sweet voice!

Keeping the view from the top in mind
The body again started moving
Challenging the uphill struggle
Screaming for the top
I again hopped

With a rediscovered energy,
Yes,
I again hopped!

Imagine the final favorable result, for which you are working so hard for, that glorious moment.

Felt good, right?

It rejuvenated you, isn't it?

That is the power of that final favorable destination!

Whenever you feel that fatigue, whenever you feel tired, just remember that final favorable destination or moment, live it for sometime. It will definitely motivate you and will provide you with the lost reservoir of energy! ☺

EPISODE 14

"Ride for desires
But,
Don't let desires ride you!"

It might happen that, to fulfill our desires, we change our attitude, our relationship, and bonding with the surrounding people, like our family or friends, with no need to do so!

We become negligent and arrogant.

Not only while working on them, but this can also happen when we have achieved our desires because we let that success of desire to get into our heads!

Hence, while working to fulfill our desires, we should keep in mind that,

We should not let our desires dictate how we behave; we should work to fulfill our desires based on how we naturally behave and don't let those desires get into our heads!

You were supposed to be the sorcerer
And I was supposed to be the object
But,
When the time of show came nearby
Why did you disappear?
Like you were the object!

And so, begins the battle of a lifetime between two powerful voices!

EPISODE 15

Once upon a time
There was a heated argument going on,
Between dear heart
And
Dear mind,
Where, dear heart,
Was saying,

"I am in favor of love, of care, of affection.
Whenever I say
I love that girl or boy
Soo cute,
Let's find out more
Let's do this
As I want to
I know you will not let that happen
Because every time I want something,

You put forward your stupid philosophy
You never interrupt, dear lung,
Or dear liver,
Why you do Soo???"

To which,
Dear mind responded,

"I do this for the betterment of you!
And the machine which we are carrying
I am in favor of wisdom, of reasoning.
But you,
You
Never understand
You just go on and on
Living in your so-called cute
Fantasies!
You never stop
Never listen to me!"

And so,
The argument heated
To which I said,

"Shut up, both of you!
I know whatever I say,
Will not affect you both

But listen,
Both of you are important to me!
With none of you both,
I will be useless
Both are poles apart
and
That's why you two make such a perfect pair!
Because
One will always need another to balance itself!"

Yes,

I was talking about the never-ending, lifetime battle between the voices which we have in our head and the voices which we have in our heart!

Surprised about this discovery of fresh voices?

Well, you should be, but we do have these voices living in our heart as we have them in our head.

Quite opposite to the voices in the head, these voices are gentle, are soft, these are the voices that usually float with love, affection, and care.

Because of this contrasting nature only, there is a constant tussle between both voices.

Sometimes they align, but it happens rarely, but I tell you those few moments are moments of peace!

But these moments of peace should not get prolonged or should not come very often.

Because the tussle between these two voices keeps us on the right path.

As voices from the heart easily float away and hence, we need the contrast of voices from the head to hold them.

And voices from the head are too hard-hitting, to soften which we need the contrast of voices from the heart!

There are many battlegrounds for these two voices to fight on, but

But their most beloved battleground is the arena of LOVE.

Isn't it? ☺

"Even though we are far apart

For now.

But,

We will meet soon

And

This world will rejoice

On seeing this beautiful moment

Trust me! 😉"

EPISODE 16

It is hard to decipher Love, as

For some, Love is a cute minor tragedy, it is those magical moments, while for some it is life's greatest gift!

But when you really like someone, when you really feel affectionate towards them, you become restless, as you are experiencing a new set of emotions towards them, and it may feel like a crossroads sometimes!

Crossroads…
It seems to be
Crossroads…
That is all I can see

Standing at the cross,
Where to go?
Is a big tragedy

Crossroads…
That is where I found myself to be!
Where to go?
Where to land?
Say out loud,
My little heart!

Crossroads…
Where I don't want myself to be
Crossroads…
Is all I can see!

Usually, we have two types of contrasting thoughts running in such situations: one,

"I need to tell what I feel" thought.

Second,

"What if I tell and I lose what I currently have?" thought!

Here, I used 'usually' because not everyone faces this dilemma. Some are absolutely clear about what they want to do when they find themselves in such a situation, while others are not!

And there is no such good choice or terrible choice, to be clear or not to be clear, after all, it's emotions we are talking about.

And because of this dilemma only, we find ourselves

At the cross of a CROSSROAD.

EPISODE 17

Let's assume we end up deciding to choose the road of

telling what we feel, enormous relief!

But everyone will not get an affirmative reaction in response. Some might get and some won't. It's all practical.

Let's consider the non-affirmative case first.

Some easily digest this and move on, but for some, it gets really hard to do so!

We might succeed in further attempts, but some of us

risk our self-respect and our behavior in doing so…

Just hoping to turn that negative into affirmative!

That's where we commit the gravest mistake.

In this situation, we need the balance of voices from our head, as they say,

Walk on the road of life
Keeping your head high

Sometimes, bend it low
But only for those who actually deserve it!

Life will give you many situations
But remember,
Walk with your head high
Preserve your two most valuables
Self-respect & behavior

Listen to others with the utmost respect
But,
You and only you know
If your behavior is right or wrong,
And whether you really need to
implement what they say!

No need to change
If you can deliver,
Keeping your attitude intact
And without hurting others!

These two are your prized possessions
Self-respect & behavior!
Never lose them

They are not monetary,
They are not for sale!

As I told you earlier, voices from the head are hard, and we need them to counterbalance the soft voices from the heart.

It's not like if a response is in denial, then the person is wrong, and hence we don't need to bend, ***Nooooo!***

The person has every right to make their own decision. We just don't need to bend in such a situation because we never know when we cross the line of losing our self-respect, and hence, we need to be cautious.

We end up chasing someone so much that we end up hurting our self-respect and with no need for it; we change our behavior, according to them, even though we know we are behaving correctly!

We need to remember,

Nothing and no one is and will be greater than our self-respect and if we know our behavior is correct,

then let people like you back as you are, no need to change for anyone and anything!

WE ARE
'NOT FOR SALE'
!!!

EPISODE 18

Flamboyant love
Once asked to the unconscious heart…

"Hey unconscious!
What is your situation these days?"

To which,
The heart gently smiled and responded.

"Hey, love!
It's really you,
Who is asking me that?
At one point, I cry.
I laugh at another.
At this point, I may be shaky.
And at another, I may be calm and silent
Oh, dear love,

Is it actually you?
Who is inquiring about my situation?
Sometimes I am lost in her memory
And sometimes,
I become desperate only to talk with her!
But,
Whenever I talk with her,
I either just jump off and dance
Or,
I just sit quietly, concentrating on her words
Dude!
I, myself, don't even know my situation
What should I tell you?
Hey love,
Now you only tell me,
Do I control my situation?
Or,
For now,
You are the only master of my situation!
Hey love,
Now you only tell me!
Now,
You only explain to me!"

EPISODE 19

Remember?

When I told you, how important is the fight between the voices from the head and heart?

How do they balance each other?

Like a bee
Trapped in a spider web
My heart,
dear heart,
Is also trapped in a web

Like a bee
Buzzing and fidgeting
To get out of the web
My heart also buzzes!

Buzzes,
Sometimes to get out
And sometimes,
Just to remain there
Unlike the bee.

Like a bee,
Tired and drained
From the struggle
My heart,
dear heart,
Just suddenly becomes calm and peaceful
Befriending the situation

But,
dear heart,
Just like the bee
Again, starts buzzing!

What to say?
The bee and my heart
dear heart,
Seem to be distinct relatives!
But,
For the bee
The fate of being eaten up
Is fixed

But
For my heart,
dear heart,
Just remain entangled there
The spider
Never appears
Or it frees up!
heart
my dear heart!

When we feel so much affection towards someone, when we are so engrossed in their thoughts, even though we know the reality, we don't want to accept it, and in that process, we end up giving more space to the voices from the heart than the ones from the head, that disturbs the balance and creates such a situation of complete entanglement.

Even though somewhere down the line we know what the voices from the head are conveying, is right, despite that, we push them back and end up,

Creating a virtual spider web for ourselves, in which we get entangled!

EPISODE 20

After we realize our mistake of letting voices from the heart overpower voices from the head, it can really shatter us for real!

Out in the mist,
She screamed,
Something wrong had happened
It seemed!

No scars
No blood,
Nothing
Only her and her regrets
Were there to scream

Rushed in emotions,
Blinded by her heart,

She took the path
Rejected by the brain, it seemed

the fight
Between the heart and the mind was on…
No physical scars
The fight had
But mental ones
Eloped under the head,
She had!

The heart won
When it shouldn't be
She took the path
She wasn't supposed to be

Which led to her doom
It's sadly true

She was not the one to let down
She was the one to stand above!

From the mistakes, she evolved.
Rising from the ashes,
She decided

To think from the brain
Even when it's heart's time
To dance in the rain!

When we realize what we have done, what was our mistake, or I should say, when the reality finally strikes hard at us,

It takes a lot of tolls on us. Sometimes we may need a lot of time to heal from that, and in those moments,

There is quite a strong chance for us to become emotionless and,

We end up deciding to shove the voices from the heart in the garbage bag!

In the hope of not committing the same mistake again.

But, instead of learning from one mistake, we end up knocking at the door of another one,

By again deciding to invite one more imbalance between the voices!

EPISODE 21

Beneath the starlight,
Of the lonely sorrows
She again found herself
Amid
Sparkling sun

Forgot the ones
Who betrayed her,
Forgot the ones
Who left her,
In the middle of
A deserted island
Where she needed them the most,

Beneath the starlight,
Of the going shadows
She took a vow

To never turn back
To never trust

Those sugar-coated people!
Who seemed to be,
Sugar inside a bitter juice
took away
Her close ones
And gave her,
A momentary disability!

Beneath the starlight,
In the reality,
She learned
She learned…

From the false starlight,
And,
Again, rose above the horizon
To see the actual starlight
And,

Live on her own
To the fullest!

"Neither Of Them Knew...
When The Season Changed
And Their Drought-Filled Lives,
Blossomed In The Presence Of Each
Other!"

Some say,

There's always pain and hardships on the path of Love!

I say,

Bullshit!

EPISODE 22

What's on your mind?
She asks…

"Peep into my mind, dear
You will find a complete section devoted to you!
And others,
others
Just Working in sync with that one.
The world says
I have gone mad for you!
In response, I just smile
And shove them away
As I know,
I know
I have not forgotten my purpose, my path,
and yours too!
But to have you alongside me on both the paths

That's my desire, and that's my wish.
When I engraved your name on my soul,
I found out that,
It was already engraved there for eternity!"

That's what I wish to respond!
That's what,
I hope
she's ready to listen!

Being in love doesn't mean talking all day, all night, spending hours thinking about each other and all.

It's all filmy!

Being in love means understanding each other, knowing each other, knowing what they like and don't, knowing each other's dreams and goals in life.

And helping them, motivating them, to achieve those!

Love doesn't mean doing all those filmy stuffs, which could distract them and yourself from the path!

Moving hand in hand, contribute to staying on the path, that's what love is!

Small, small fights are bound to happen, even so-called perfect couples don't have 100% compatibility,

But getting out together from those small spats is love!

"The Fabric Of Hope, Is Stitched
Together With...
Love, Compassion,
Togetherness &
Faith!"

"If I were a spy
I will keep a watch on my heart
As it wonders too much nowadays!"

EPISODE 23

Scrolling down the photos,
Suddenly, some sort of nostalgia came

Those were the days
Those were the time
When I had you,
And you had I

But now,
Now
We are just some lost faces in the crowd

Waking up early
Tired till evening
Sleeping at night
Now you are unrecognizable
And so am I!

We have just become
Some lost faces in the crowd

Those were the days
Those were the time
When I had you,
And you had me!

The daily hard-work routine phobia is so deadly that it can consume the love which we have within us for our loved ones.

We can't even think or feel anything except what we work hard for.

We just block everything out, including love, emotions, and feelings.

Unknowingly, we let voices in our head win over voices in our heart, which again leads to the same imbalance we have been talking about.

Hence, it is important to walk the path of love and the path of life hand in hand.

So that loved ones can save each other from

Daily hard-work routine phobia!

Today, I will take time and
Bring back those memory lanes
Which were glorified by
"us"
But which are now solitary
In absence of
"us"!

EPISODE 24

Within that smile,
You feel and you know
There is still some doubt
Some pain left

You try to remove that rust
Hoping to get that diamond back,
Multiple times,
But multiple times you fail,

Because you haven't received that broom yet
Which would help you remove that rust!
But it is you and only you
Whose sole responsibility is
To find that broom,
To get the purity of the heart

The trust back
To get the diamond back!

Then, suddenly, someday,
Via something or someone
Something kicks inside you

You find that broom!
You start removing that rust
You start feeling lightened again
You start feeling satisfied!

That day,
That moment
You are reborn!
You have again carved
that diamond back!

One of the biggest mistakes in life we make is,

Finding fault in others and blaming them for our situation!

In fact, this is the biggest fault we commit in our own life!

We ignore to accept the fact that,

We can't control other's lives, but we can control ours!

We ignore to accept the fact that,

We can't control how someone behaves, but we can control how we can!

We ignore to accept the fact that,

Nobody depends on no one!

And we still falsely believe,

How can they do that to me?

But in fact, they had done nothing wrong; they took their life's decision on their own and ***you also should!***

We ourself, have to figure out,

What is good for self, and what isn't!

Life is ours. We need to decide, hear other's opinions, adapt them if they are good and would help you, but don't rely only on them!

Similarly

For the situation we are in, we should analyze what we did good and wrong, and should not analyze what wrong and good others did.

"The Scars Which You Can Not See
Take Longest To Heal!"

EPISODE 25

With The Rising Sun
And With The Rising Sun

All The Words You Said
The Sensation Of Your Touch
The Melody Of Your Laughter
All Will Be Gone

And With The Rising Sun
With The Rising Sun,
The Shiny Glitter Of Your Eyes
Your Once Soothing Words
Your Deadly Smile
All Will Be Gone

With The Sunrise
The Memories Of Our Being As Us,

The Desire To Be Lifelong
All Will Be Faded
All Will Be Gone!
The Holding Of Hands
The Whisper Of Secrets
The Thrilling Hideouts,
Will Be All Gone
With The First Ray Of The Morning Sun
With The First Appearance Of The Morning Sun!

But Before The Morning Sun
Dear,
Before The Morning Sun
What Have We Done
To Each Other…?
What Not Have We Said
To Each Other…?

Dear,
Before The Morning Sun
I Wish,
I Just Wish
I Had A Time Machine
To Erase It All!
To Be With You With The Morning Sun!

What Have We Done To Each Other?

Dear,
What Not Have We Said To Each Other?
I Wish,
I Just Wish
I Could Erase It All!

With The Morning Sun
But,
My Dear
With The Morning Sun
How Can I Erase The Care?
The Care Which I Had And Will Have For You!
How Can I Erase It?
Please Tell Me!

With The Morning Sun
Even Without Saying
I Will Hear Your Voice
In Need Of Help,
In Need Of Guidance
How That Can Be Erased?
Please Guide Me

With The Morning Sun
I Can't Erase That Care
My Dear
I Can't

I'm Sorry!

I Will Be There
Disguised,
In Some Form Or Another
I Will Be There

Before The Morning Sun
What Have We Done To Each Other…?
What Not Have We Said To Each Other…?
My Dear,
I Wish I Could Erase
I Wish We Could Go Back!

There will always be certain moments in life that we want to erase, or which we want to re-do for a better outcome, but unfortunately, we can't!

We have to live with those.

In these situations, we usually have 2 options,

Either we entirely try to suppress our past and hide it completely somewhere within us.

Or we can come out with our past in the open and freely talk about it.

It entirely depends on the situation.

If your past only hurts you, only takes you back a few steps each time, then it's better to deal with it and suppress it somewhere within ourselves, or

If remembering your past once in a while gives you strength, gives you power, always teaches you something, then there's no harm in remembering it sometimes. Of course, it will hurt a bit, but the power, the learning, the courage, which you will get, will help you overcome that momentary hurt and will help you fight back distinct problems in life.

"True Power,

Is Not In Pretending To Be

Who You Are Not!

But,

In Admitting The Truth

Who You Are!"

EPISODE 26

Have you ever in your life, felt so close to someone, be it any kind of relationship, that talking to them made you feel peaceful, made you feel safe, but because of any reason, be it because of misunderstandings or some natural reasons, that someone departed away from you, and equations never became same again?

Have you?

With the first drop of rain of the season
Which you will experience in your consciousness
You will feel my presence
Dear
With the first drop of rain of the season
Which you will experience in your consciousness
You will feel my presence

Standing beside you,
Hand in hand,
Giving you,
Your well-deserved energy

With the first drop of rain of the season
Which you will experience in your consciousness
You will feel my presence
Hand in hand,
Rejuvenating you!

Just like flower blossom with a touch of rain
After experiencing dry heat,
Dear,
I will be there!

Said she before leaving him

And from that day onwards,
Each year,
He waits for the first drop of rain
Which he could experience

To feel her,
To be with her,
For one more time,
To survive another year till the next rain

With the touch
The energy she provided

With the first drop of rain
Which He experienced in his consciousness!

We all are different. We have different thoughts, different feelings, different behavior, and whatnot!

But I feel somewhere down the line, we all want one thing,

To meet someone, to get in touch with someone, with whom we can share our thoughts, our feelings, our emotions, even our anger openly, with no hesitation, and they also feel the same level of safety towards us.

With whom we can have open mutual communication on any topic, without thinking twice.

With whom we can even fight, but in the end, we get back together.

Whose, we can pull the legs freely and so does that person!

It may sound like I'm talking about a romantic relationship, but trust me, I'm not!

Apart from a romantic relationship, we can achieve these things via friendship. Even mentor-mentee can have a similar bond!

But, when that person leaves us, departs away from us, because of whatever reason, it hurts…

It hurts deeply!

It leaves a hole somewhere, whose pain we might decrease, but we cannot fill that hole!

And hence, sometimes, to regain the energy, to remember the bond, we have to stay in touch with the beautiful memories we share with them!

EPISODE 27

As I told you earlier, voices from the head and voices from the heart can come in sync, even though it shouldn't last for long, but it happens!

It can happen in many scenarios, like when you are still and just observing something, thinking, maybe something happy, maybe something sad, but you are thinking, that can prove to be that moment when

Voices from the head and form heart come into sync!

Standing barefoot
On the sand of the beach
Observing the water,
Flowing from a distance,
Coming towards me,
Touching my barefoot
And again retreating

I sensed
A known behavior

The unfortunate odyssey of life
Of people coming and going

Standing barefoot
On the sand of the beach
I wanted the stream of water to stay
I wanted to behold it
In a friendly grasp till infinity,

But it went by
Leaving me there,
Waiting for it to come back
It felt like a sad odyssey of life
Of people coming and going!

I wanted them to stay
I wanted them to stand alongside me
Just like I
Wished to stand alongside them

I wanted to behold to them
In a friendly
Loving grasp till infinity!

Standing barefoot
On the sand of the beach
Waiting for the stream
Observing its every flow,
Every move
And it came,
It never disappoints me
It comes back
And hence the eager wait feels like bliss!

Standing barefoot
On the sand of the beach
Reminded me
Of the eagerly wait I did
For the people who moved on
Leaving me there,
Just like the stream of water
But,

Unlike the stream,
Who comes back,
They rarely come back
Leaving a void

A void
Only to be
filled with time
And time only!

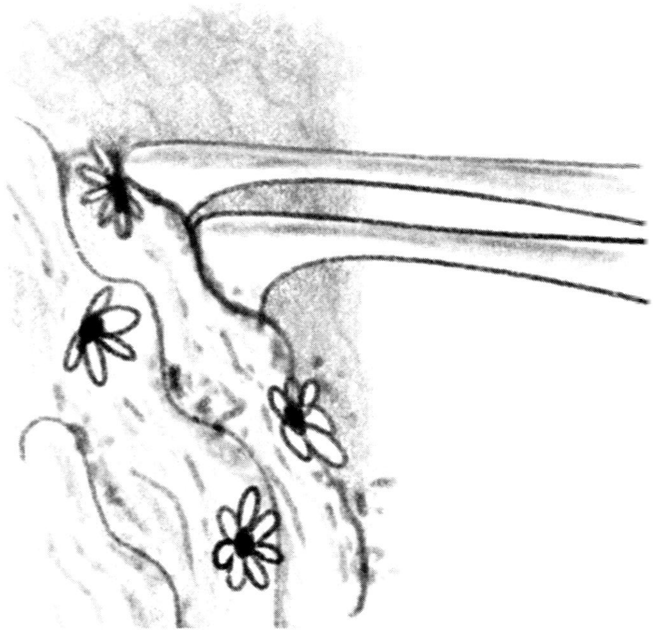

THE END

'Voices' convey many things,

Some which I get delighted to hear and some which I never want to hear!

But these voices are always there, to guide me, to help me, to accompany me.

It's not like these voices are always right,

Hence, these voices are present in a pair, to balance each other!

Voices from head

&

Voices from heart

These two are like siblings,

Constantly fighting, arguing, cutting each other out,

But when one fails, the other one is there to take the front stand!

Sometimes, both of them get in sync and that's when I get some moment of peace!

But if they don't argue over a long period,

Then it's a sign that something's wrong because If they don't argue, I might act just in free will, which may lead to doom!

Hence, both of them are important to me.

So, this was the story of my voices,

And what they conveyed till now and how they will continue to do so!

Hope it helps you to find and befriend yours,

If you haven't till now ☺

And just remember one thing in and about life,

Life is a brilliant teacher,
We just need to be excellent students!

It's SOOOOOO Simple,

Isn’t it? 😉

Greetings from the Author

"Hello, reader friends!

If you have reached till here, then I hope you have read the content and haven't jumped directly to this page!

If you have already read or will read, I wish you have a great reading experience and I'm eagerly waiting to read and receive your reviews!

Let me tell you something about myself, apart from the stuff which you might have already guessed from the write-up.

So, I had started my writing journey around the last year of my graduation. What struck me in those days, whether any coconut fell on my head or I banged my head on the coconut, so that I suddenly started writing, God knows!

But I did, and here I'm presenting my book to you all.

I was born and brought up in the cleanest city of India, Indore, which was not that clean when I was born, but not because I was born!

Completed my graduation in a neighboring city, not that neighboring actually, Bhopal, and then finally settled in Pune, before venturing a bit in Chennai, as part of a Software Development job.

When I started my writing journey, I used to write some articles, primarily based on current affairs of our country. From there on I transitioned into a blogger, adding short story writing into my kitty along the way.

Then one fine day, the coconut again appeared suddenly and again whether it fell on my head or I banged my head on it, I started writing poetry!

Since then, the journey has never stopped. It slows down a bit for evaluation, but it didn't come to a halt, as I started trying out thing after another in the literary field.

Be it content writing, book reviews, stage shows, poetry recitations, and the latest, writing and publishing my book.

I majorly write in Hindi and English languages and have a wish to learn more beautiful languages and especially write in my mother tongue, i.e., Marathi.

Apart from this, just to keep between you and me, I do have a desire to be a theater artist as well.

Again, hope you like the content and waiting for your priceless reviews.

Until next time!"

Few Words by the Illustrator!

"Hello, reader friends!

I'm your illustrator Priya, hope you found the illustrations relatable, intriguing and entertaining, at the same time!

Well, this was my very first venture, being an illustrator, and there are quite a few areas for improvement, which you might have also noticed.

I'm a learner and I like to experiment, learn and grow.

Nobody is born an artist, we need to identify our passion and likings, and work on them as we grow.

This is exactly what I did when I started on this self-taught journey towards becoming an artist, along with these beautiful colors.

I found a social media companion along the way, in the form of Instagram, as I realized its potential to help me learn from other's art and at the same time, allow my art to reach others.

I started depicting real-life incidents in a fun-filled and relatable way via doodles on Instagram.

Most recently I fell in love with watercolors again, as I started with therapeutic watercolor paintings and experiments.

The artistic world has no boundaries and hence I'm continuing the journey in this world with new and exciting art forms like paint making, pottery, terrariums, plants, sculpting, jewelry, homemade cosmetics, and more.

I once again wish that you found the illustrations relatable, intriguing and entertaining, at the same time.

You can reach out to me on my Instagram page - @aquaraltheropy

Until next time!"

Acknowledgement

I must admit, this section is tougher to write than the main content itself!

Especially when the book is about the learnings which you have received throughout your life. As so many people impact us directly and indirectly, so many are involved in these learnings.

But it's always a good practice to include this part, to convey gratitude, so if anyone gets left out, heartfelt apologies to them.

So where to start?

Of course, from the family, the support, the motivation, the learnings which they continue to provide is unparallel.

Every ounce of gratitude is less in their case.

Moving on to this book's illustrator, you all know her name, no need for an introduction. Having no prior experience in doing illustrations, she believed in the content and did an amazing job for the book.

Namrata Bheemge, for taking out time from her busy schedule, to help in editing the first couple of drafts of the book.

The entire team of Blue Rose Publishers, for keeping faith in my content and helping me out on my first publishing journey.

The one source of energy, which kept on pushing me to write and write and never give up, was the words spoken by Anil Deshmukh, my ex-colleague and senior, when in his farewell he said to all, pointing towards me - *You all will one day proudly say that we worked with this writer, this man!*

Thank you, Anil, for those words and faith.

Vishal Ranjan, for his never-ending, continuous pieces of advice, which I hope will never end!

Kapil Kumar has no interest in reading, but is a dear friend and his continuous banter, humor, and friendly guidance keeps me at bay.

Abhishek Raikwar, Damini Sehgal, Mohit Kulkarni, for all the learnings and fun moments, right from the time when we started our corporate lives together, till recent past.

My school buddies, Anirudha Dixit, Kapil Devatwal, Rachit Porwal, Shashank Patankar, Varun Khargonkar & Vipin Joshi. The bond remains vital.

I started this section with my family and I will end it with my other family, my brothers, my college buddies, you all rock!

Shivam Agarwal, Shubham Jain, Shubham Shukla (also a writer and continues to help me with my Hindi content), Sumeet Verma, Vivek Sharma & Zaid Kamali, thank you for being there despite all the ups and downs.

Again, if I missed anyone, heartfelt apologies, you will be covered next time!